SEASON SEARCH

A SPOT-IT CHALLENGE

by Sarah L. Schuette

CAPSTONE PRESS
a capstone imprint

A+
books

A+ Books are published by Capstone Press,
151 Good Counsel Drive, P.O. Box 669, Mankato, Minnesota 56002.
www.capstonepub.com

 Books published by Capstone Press are manufactured with paper
containing at least 10 percent post-consumer waste.

Library of Congress Cataloging-in-Publication Data
Schuette, Sarah L., 1976–
  Season search : a spot-it challenge / by Sarah L. Schuette.
    p. cm.—(Spot it)
  Includes bibliographical references.
  Summary: "Simple text invites the reader to find items hidden in seasonal-themed photographs"—
Provided by publisher.
  ISBN 978-1-4296-5261-2 (library binding)
  1. Puzzles. 2. Picture puzzles—Juvenile literature. [1. Picture puzzles. 2. Puzzles.] I. Title. II. Series.
  GV1507.P47S38 2011
  793.73—dc22   2010044162

Credits

Jenny Marks and Erika L. Shores, editors; Ted Williams, designer; Juliette Peters, set designer;
Eric Manske, production specialist; Sarah Schuette, photo stylist; Marcy Morin, photo scheduler

Photo Credits

all photos by Capstone Studio/Karon Dubke

Note to Parents, Teachers, and Librarians

Spot It is an interactive series that supports literacy development and reading enjoyment.
Readers utilize visual discrimination skills to find objects among fun-to-peruse photographs
with busy backgrounds. Readers also build vocabulary through thematic groupings, develop
visual memory ability through repeated readings, and improve strategic and associative
thinking skills by experimenting with different visual search methods.

The author dedicates this book to her goddaughter, Muriel Hilgers.

Printed in the United States of America in North Mankato, Minnesota.
092010   005933CGS11

Table of Contents

Showers & Flowers

Can you spot . . .

- a zebra?
- two tadpoles?
- a spray bottle?
- a gift bag?
- a head of lettuce?
- a cactus?

5

Lucky You

Can you spot . . .

- a hay bale?
- a grasshopper?
- a dragon?
- a horse?
- a robot?
- two aliens?

6

Camp Out

Can you spot . . .

- a buffalo?
- a dollar sign?
- a telescope?
- a chain saw?
- a flashlight?
- a laptop?

Summertime Scoops

Can you spot . . .

- a celery stick?
- a screw?
- a crown?
- a butterfly?
- two pretzels?
- a cake?

Fun in the Sun

Can you spot . . .

- a stop sign?
- a swan?
- a spider?
- a pumpkin?
- a donut?
- a skateboard?

12

Parade

Can you spot . . .
- a flamingo?
- a lawn mower?
- a bathtub?
- a waste basket?
- a hot air balloon?
- a box of tomatoes?

15

School Days

Can you spot . . .

- a gumball machine?
- a tuba?
- a hamburger?
- a dolphin?
- a whoopee cushion?
- a football jersey?

18

Apples

Can you spot . . .

- a turkey?
- a lantern?
- two hot dogs?
- a toolbox?
- two fishing bobbers?
- two lions?

Gobble!

Can you spot . . .

- a flip flop?
- a drum?
- an octopus?
- a bucket?
- a tugboat?
- a row of ghosts?

Snow & Ice

Can you spot . . .

- a push pin?
- a dragonfly?
- a megaphone?
- a web?
- two poodles?
- a moon?

23

President's Day

Can you spot . . .

- an elephant?
- two axes?
- two briefcases?
- an iron?
- a pair of binoculars?
- a sandwich?

Love You

Can you spot . . .

- a white rabbit?
- a bell?
- a lamp?
- a key?
- two shoes?
- two dresses?

Spot Even More!

Showers & Flowers

Try to find two shamrocks, a barrel, a Christmas tree, a jackhammer, and four birdhouses.

Lucky You

Now spot three doves, a palm tree, a pirate, and a bunch of bananas.

Camp Out

Now find an ear of corn, a crutch, a steak, a hammer, two airplanes, and two rolls of duct tape.

Summertime Scoops

Try to find a bone, three ice cream sandwiches, a nail, two polar bears, and two snowflakes.

Fun in the Sun

Try to find a boot, a pair of sunglasses, an anchor, and a water canteen.

Parade

Try to spot a baby, a TV, a pencil, and a horse with wings.

School Days

See if you can spot four apple slices, two pieces of cauliflower, a blue eraser, and a spoon.

Apples

Now spot a baseball cap, a sink, a raccoon, an angel, and a baseball bat.

Gobble!

See if you can find three suns, a gnome, a race car, a bowling pin, and two goldfish.

Snow & Ice

Now look for a train engine, two Eiffel Towers, a cow, and a blackberry.

President's Day

Take another look to find a witch's hat, a scissors, a shovel, and a wrench.

Love You

This time find a toaster, a golf tee, a staple, a nail file, and a whistle.

Extreme Spot-It Challenge

Just can't get enough Spot-It action?
Here's an extra challenge. Try to spot:

- a mermaid
- a rooster
- two traffic cones
- a helicopter
- an ambulance
- a squirrel
- a grill
- a potato chip
- a broom
- a strawberry
- a fairy wand
- a toilet
- Santa's hat
- a pocket watch
- a mouse with cheese
- two astronauts
- a tennis racket

Read More

Chedru, Delphine. *Spot It Again!: Find More Hidden Creatures.* New York: Abrams Books for Young Readers, 2011.

Marks, Jennifer L. *Christmas Fun: A Spot-It Challenge.* Spot It. Mankato, Minn.: Capstone Press, 2009.

Internet Sites

FactHound offers a safe, fun way to find Internet sites related to this book. All of the sites on FactHound have been researched by our staff.

Here's all you do:

Visit *www.facthound.com*

Type in this code: **9781429652612**

 Check out projects, games and lots more at
www.capstonekids.com